Epic
Whizz Inc™
publishing

The Singing Clouds

SEBASTIAN J. H. JUNG

Introduction

Children have the ability to feel, learn, and create their own stories through their senses. When we look at the world we live in through the eyes of children, every raindrop, puddle of water, and rainbow that blooms in the sky becomes curious, exciting, and fun. In this book, the rhythmic and cheerful sounds of rain and rainfall are expressed in a synesthetic way through children's laughter, musical scores, and the love conveyed through rain. And through its beautiful illustrations, the book stimulates the senses and imagination of children who read it, helping them develop their emotions, sensibilities, and creativity. It also helps children appreciate the beauty of the world they live in and the things around them.

Since it is not raining, the ground, trees, and animal friends in the forest are all feeling thirsty.

Somewhere, a cool wind is blowing through the dry sky,

drawing the five lines of a musical score.

And with that wind come clouds full of love.

"Rumble, boom, boom!" Lightning and thunder fall to the ground, creating high, low, and diatonic clefs.

And the raindrops, carrying the love that the clouds have, travel along the lines the wind has made, moistening the parched earth.

The raindrops sing to make a beautiful harmony with the leaves, stones, and stagnant water.

Shall we listen too?

What sounds do you hear?

After a bout of chorus, the dried-up forest regained its shiny green color.

The rainbow shines brightly and applauds them for singing well.

Today, what does it seem like in the city we live in?

It is full of various pollutants, including exhaust fumes produced by cars and factories.

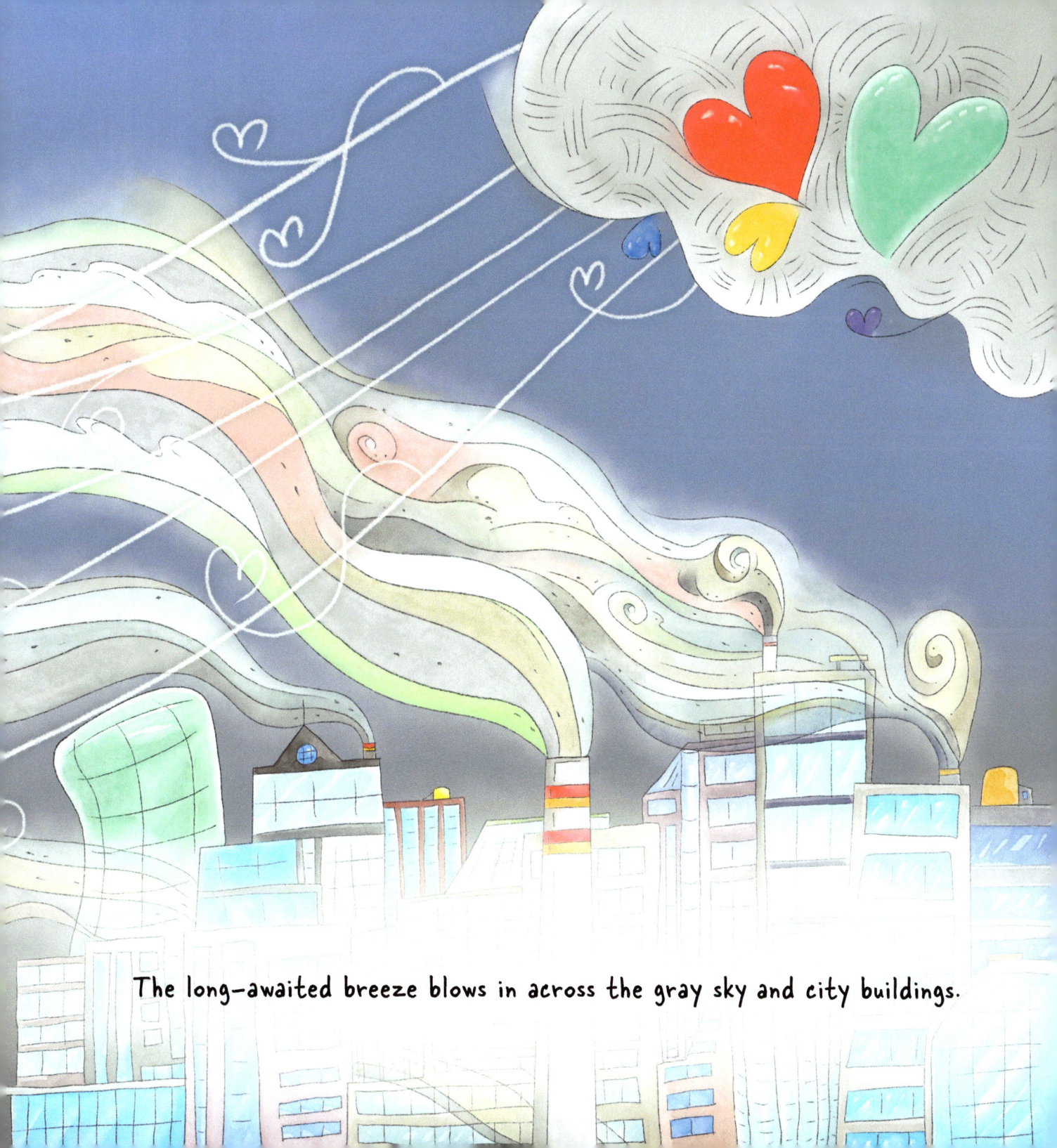

The long-awaited breeze blows in across the gray sky and city buildings.

And a prelude composed of notes is played even over the gray city.

"Rumble, boom, boom!"

After a while, raindrops come down, singing and conveying the love of
the clouds along the stave made by the wind and musical notes.

The raindrops fall on roofs, on parked cars, on a discarded crushed can, and even on the head of a cat that goes for a walk outside, forming various harmonies and composing songs.

Shall we listen too?

What sounds do you hear?

A car passing through stagnant rainwater
and the raindrops falling on the umbrellas
where people are walking—these all sound
like a melody for a harmonized, beautiful
song of love.

Shall we listen too?

What sounds do you hear?

Raindrops fall on the children returning home to convey the love of the clouds. And when they meet the children's umbrellas and raincoats, a song is created in beautiful harmony.

Shall we listen too?

What sounds do you hear?

The gray sky and city became clean with the sound of beautiful singing. Rainbow, who heard the song, applauds brilliantly and smiles, saying that they did a great job.

Shall we clap together too?

Even today, on this earth where we all live, there are many beautiful sounds, like the singing clouds that convey the love of Jesus Christ.

Shall we listen to what these are?

What sounds do you hear?

Author's Note

One day, when rain was pounding on the window, I suddenly had this thought.
What if young readers could imagine the sound of rain through a picture book?
I thought it could be a fun participatory activity for children.
While drawing the drifting clouds, I remembered a sentence: "The rain falls to
ride love." So, I drew some heart-fluttering clouds with heart symbols. And winds
became the musical staves, and thunder and lighting became the high, low, and
diatonic clefs. Then the falling raindrops became notes singing along the wind's
musical staves.
Therefore, I illustrated them playing music in harmony when they touched the
ground.
I wanted to express sound through the illustrations in this picture book.

You listened to the song of the rain.
What sounds did you hear?
I hope that it will be a good time for not only children but also parents to express
their creative ideas in a fun way.

First Edition, 2024

ISBN: 978-1-989748-52-7

ISBN: 978-1-989748-51-0 (eBook)

www.epicwhizz.com

www.animahero.com